JJMG Enterprises LLC

Question Vault

450 Practice Verbal Questions for the SSAT® Upper

Question Vault

450 Practice Verbal Questions for the SSAT® Upper

Justin Grosslight

Published by JJMG Enterprises LLC

Editorial:
Justin Grosslight, head author

JJMG Enterprises LLC
30 N. Gould St.
Suite N
Sheridan, WY 82801
USA

ISBN: 978-0-9974232-5-9

10 9 8 7 6 5 4 3 2 1

Note that SSAT is a registered trademark of the Secondary School Admission Test Board, which neither sponsors nor endorses this product.

TABLE OF CONTENTS:

WHAT IS THE PURPOSE OF THIS BOOK?

Preparing for the verbal section of the SSAT can be a challenging task for many students, particularly if their vocabulary repertoire is limited (this is especially true for international students whose first language is not English). The English language contains tens of thousands of words, and guessing which ones will appear on the SSAT can be a tough task. This book is intended to provide you with exposure to several hundred words that have frequently appeared on exams for high school admissions and college admissions tests. Practicing the questions contained in this text is a good means of learning new and exciting words.

This book has been written in response to the success of *Verbal Boot Camp for the SSAT Upper*. In response to the demand for more questions, we have provided an entirely new bank of practice questions here. For those preparing for the SSAT, this book hopefully satisfies your desires.

At the same time, we realize that practicing questions should be just part of a regimen to improve one's vocabulary. Often students begin preparing for the SSAT verbal exam too late and are forced to cram long lists of words in a short time – only to forget many of the words after the exam is over. Complementing practice questions with sustained, active reading of intellectual and/or academic materials (not from school textbooks) is the best way to improve one's vocabulary. These habits, combined with regular review of vocabulary – flash cards can be a good idea – often produce the best results. As for this book, it is intended for anyone seeking a verbal workout challenge, especially for students in grades 8 through 10 who plan to take the SSAT upper exam.

A note to consider: many of the words on the SSAT verbal exam are very difficult and are well above an early high school vocabulary level. Parents should not panic about performances from this book or on test day itself that seem out of step with their child's abilities. Though SSAT scores are important, the application process to private American boarding schools is holistic and considers grades, interviews, essays, recommendations, extracurricular activities, and other factors as part of the admissions process. Nonetheless, with proper practice, guidance and encouragement, anybody can improve his or her chances of SSAT success.

SYNONYMS

Each of the following questions consists of one word followed by five words or phrases. You are to select the one word or phrase whose meaning is closest to the word in capital letters.

1. RECTIFY

(A) concoct
(B) correct
(C) alter
(D) damage
(E) confuse

2. BREACH

(A) violation
(B) shrill sound
(C) inclination
(D) stretch
(E) jump

3. COMEBACK

(A) to take a recess
(B) to destroy
(C) to joke
(D) to return to activity
(E) to repeat a task

4. IMPRESS

(A) to make one feel admiration and respect
(B) to make one feel scared and lonely
(C) to make one feel confused
(D) to make one feel satiated
(E) to offend

5. FORMIDABLE

(A) respectful
(B) fierce
(C) pleasant
(D) moldable
(E) compelling

6. MELODRAMATIC

(A) magnetic
(B) stoic
(C) nonchalant
(D) pleasing
(E) overemotional

7. RENDEZVOUS

(A) display
(B) secret
(C) mass upheaval
(D) covenant
(E) meeting place

8. SCOURGE

(A) curse
(B) examination
(C) rudeness
(D) levity
(E) enthusiasm

9. INTRICATE

(A) minimal
(B) brave
(C) complex
(D) thin
(E) large

10. ASSOCIATE

(A) elongate
(B) confuse
(C) wreck
(D) correlate
(E) juxtapose

11. CONNOTATION

(A) undertone
(B) lexicon
(C) structure
(D) definition
(E) etymology

12. COMMODIOUS

(A) narrow
(B) capacious
(C) angular
(D) enchanted
(E) claustrophobic

13. NOTICE

(A) glare
(B) observe
(C) forget
(D) think
(E) worry

14. CONTRADICT

(A) to change and go in the opposite direction
(B) to deny the truth of a statement
(C) to go well together
(D) to make a bad mistake
(E) to omit something from an argument

15. SUFFICE

(A) to be lacking
(B) to be filling
(C) to be optional
(D) to be necessary
(E) to be adequate

16. EUPHORIA

(A) ennui
(B) ecstasy
(C) joviality
(D) dourness
(E) indifference

17. LEVITY

(A) chemistry
(B) enmity
(C) gravity
(D) frivolity
(E) solemnity

18. MORES

(A) cards
(B) documents
(C) customs
(D) utensils
(E) losses

19. CONSTANT

(A) varying
(B) mercurial
(C) unswerving
(D) ascending
(E) tortuous

20. ACCOMMODATE

(A) to provide space for
(B) to make obstacles for
(C) to be jealous of
(D) to query
(E) to transport goods for

21. CAVORT

(A) French dessert
(B) bed sheet
(C) small desk
(D) excited dance
(E) hiding place

22. PRIOR

(A) consequential
(B) previous
(C) simultaneous
(D) posthumous
(E) annexed

23. MERCY

(A) insensitivity
(B) greatness
(C) humility
(D) craziness
(E) compassion

24. SECLUDE

(A) fear
(B) exist
(C) hide
(D) cover
(E) deny

25. TEXTURE

(A) stability
(B) complexity
(C) consistency
(D) intrigue
(E) normalcy

26. URGE

(A) warn
(B) exhort
(C) caution
(D) admonish
(E) address

27. DURABLE

(A) fragile
(B) enduring
(C) plastic
(D) mutable
(E) wobbly

28. LETHARGIC

(A) cleansing
(B) lethal
(C) torpid
(D) energetic
(E) disorganized

29. DOUSE

(A) soak
(B) dry
(C) comb
(D) raze
(E) construct

30. DOMESTIC

(A) public
(B) tame
(C) sleepy
(D) foreign
(E) national

31. BENEFICIAL

(A) alarming
(B) helpful
(C) cheerful
(D) hurtful
(E) emancipated

32. POMPOUS

(A) reserved
(B) quiet
(C) arrogant
(D) simple
(E) courteous

33. PECULIAR

(A) didactic
(B) particular
(C) generalizable
(D) disorganized
(E) sharp

34. MELANCHOLY

(A) glad
(B) bad
(C) triumphant
(D) sleepy
(E) sad

35. ASSUME

(A) bewilder
(B) thrash
(C) lavish
(D) presume
(E) harm

36. SIMULATE

(A) photocopy
(B) imitate
(C) develop
(D) twist
(E) stimulate

37. AESTHETIC

(A) concerning locations of events
(B) concerning restaurants
(C) concerning strength of materials
(D) concerning art or beauty
(E) concerning historical incidents

38. TREK

(A) sojourn
(B) expedition
(C) repetition
(D) meal
(E) jogging path

39. NOVICE

(A) book
(B) beginner
(C) entryway
(D) veteran
(E) perpetual

40.   PLIGHT

(A)   plane trip
(B)   not heavy
(C)   entry
(D)   dilemma
(E)   stamina

41.   OBLIGE

(A)   reduce
(B)   excite
(C)   respect
(D)   intrigue
(E)   compel

42.   JOVIAL

(A)   jejune
(B)   morose
(C)   harsh
(D)   stationary
(E)   affable

43.   IDEAL

(A)   creative thought
(B)   difficult situation
(C)   optimal
(D)   questionable
(E)   embarrassing

44.   CULTURE

(A)   lifestyle
(B)   hobbies
(C)   work hours
(D)   location
(E)   fears

45.   GESTURE

(A)   advice
(B)   signal
(C)   warning
(D)   incident
(E)   appliance

46.   LINCHPIN

(A)   extraneous
(B)   informal
(C)   keystone
(D)   bystander
(E)   witness

47.   FATE

(A)   health
(B)   destiny
(C)   birth
(D)   viewpoint
(E)   scale

48.   OPINION

(A)   anxiety
(B)   nostalgia for something
(C)   worry
(D)   destruction
(E)   judgment

49.   ASTUTE

(A)   obtuse
(B)   shrewd
(C)   flat
(D)   innovative
(E)   dull

50.   WITHSTAND

(A)   struggle
(B)   harm
(C)   construct
(D)   tolerate
(E)   crumble

51.   SWAGGER

(A)   to cry intensely
(B)   to walk insolently
(C)   to work industriously
(D)   to cheat sneakily
(E)   to win dishonestly

52.   MEDLEY

(A)   layering
(B)   garden
(C)   mixture
(D)   flattening
(E)   overture

53.   SCARCE

(A)   uncommon
(B)   terrifying
(C)   unknown
(D)   ubiquitous
(E)   bruise

54.   GENERATE

(A)   create
(B)   clarify
(C)   stratify
(D)   demolish
(E)   rebuild

55. DEFICIENCY

(A) well-functioning
(B) surplus
(C) lack
(D) explosive
(E) crumbling

56. ANNUL

(A) arrange
(B) officiate
(C) invalidate
(D) appraise
(E) waste

57. CRISIS

(A) detente
(B) fiasco
(C) incarceration
(D) funeral
(E) warfare

58. COLLABORATE

(A) collate
(B) thicken
(C) trace
(D) cooperate
(E) relinquish

59. GAPE

(A) touch
(B) spoil
(C) listen
(D) talk
(E) gawk

60. PESTER

(A) grind
(B) tease
(C) annoy
(D) drink
(E) sew

61. UNCANNY

(A) unusual
(B) treasonous
(C) derivative
(D) antithetical
(E) identical

62. ARTICULATE

(A) hilarious
(B) vibrant
(C) stylish
(D) musical
(E) well-spoken

63. WARY

(A) lugubrious
(B) cautious
(C) lugubrious
(D) inane
(E) combative

64. LAMENT

(A) commemorate
(B) enthrall
(C) constrain
(D) ponder
(E) mourn

65. PLEDGE

(A) vow
(B) necessitate
(C) commend
(D) abjure
(E) rebuff

66. ABASE

(A) to score in baseball
(B) to conquer
(C) to return home
(D) to behave as if to deprive someone of self-esteem
(E) to make wicked

67. STRENUOUS

(A) nutty
(B) alarming
(C) muscular
(D) taxing
(E) passive

68. REMISS

(A) absurd
(B) solitary
(C) grave
(D) situational
(E) thoughtless

69. FORTIFY

(A) dismantle
(B) sap
(C) stymie
(D) reduce
(E) strengthen

70. EXHILIRATE

(A) redress
(B) baffle
(C) excite
(D) loosen
(E) petrify

71. MANUFACTURE

(A) fabricate
(B) disown
(C) evolve
(D) inoculate
(E) erase

72. PERSONABLE

(A) amicable
(B) humanistic
(C) comatose
(D) putrid
(E) hostile

73. COMMERCE

(A) rights
(B) trade
(C) gender equality
(D) sleuthing
(E) divorce

74. DIVERT

(A) flavor
(B) distract
(C) epitomize
(D) redirect
(E) do something offensive

75. PORTENT

(A) information of high value
(B) sewer
(C) loophole
(D) omen
(E) hidden pathway

76. TRIUMPH

(A) amusement
(B) rehabilitation
(C) celebration
(D) roar
(E) manifestation

77. INIQUITY

(A) protection
(B) sin
(C) downturn
(D) pining
(E) justice

78. INHIBIT

(A) propel
(B) blame
(C) stoke
(D) increase
(E) prevent

79. TANGIBLE

(A) potable
(B) formidable
(C) touchable
(D) edible
(E) fungible

80. APEX

(A) sharp point
(B) curve
(C) canyon
(D) acme
(E) nadir

81. SOVEREIGN

(A) employee
(B) priest
(C) manager
(D) monarch
(E) janitor

82. INCENTIVE

(A) inducement
(B) thrashing
(C) order
(D) rebuttal
(E) confession

83. PROCURE

(A) to heal
(B) to object
(C) to perform
(D) to succeed
(E) to obtain

84. RESCIND

(A) to revoke
(B) to concur
(C) to howl
(D) to frame
(E) to send again

85. MAR

(A) heal
(B) bleed
(C) polish
(D) damage
(E) explode

86. PROLOGUE

(A) preface
(B) expert
(C) spoiler
(D) trainer
(E) record

87. THAW

(A) congeal
(B) understand
(C) reflect
(D) wash
(E) defrost

88. REQUEST

(A) investigation
(B) command
(C) journey
(D) inquiry
(E) inventory

89. VENT

(A) let out
(B) dismiss
(C) brood
(D) wind
(E) dissolve

90. DONATE

(A) retract
(B) give
(C) collect
(D) bake
(E) usurp

91. PUTRID

(A) cheerful
(B) quick
(C) rotten
(D) mystified
(E) disoriented

92. CONSTRUE

(A) behave
(B) believe
(C) outline
(D) dismiss
(E) interpret

93. CALLOUS

(A) bumpy
(B) rewarding
(C) insensitive
(D) bemusing
(E) guileless

94. RATIFY

(A) boost
(B) establish
(C) detach
(D) implore
(E) retreat

95. SHIRK

(A) to tremble
(B) to laugh
(C) to deviate
(D) to rattle
(E) to avoid responsibility

96. ADVOCATE

(A) witness
(B) apostate
(C) nonbeliever
(D) supporter
(E) referee

97. ELOCUTION

(A) articulation
(B) flair
(C) smarminess
(D) authenticity
(E) emotion

98. UNDERLYING

(A) subversive
(B) muddy
(C) fundamental
(D) romantic
(E) forgotten

99. DIVISIVE

(A) dissenting
(B) unanimous
(C) partial
(D) piecemeal
(E) proportional

100. DOSE

(A) yawn
(B) law enforcement agent
(C) country dance
(D) portion
(E) light sleep

101. NEWFANGLED

(A) snarled
(B) recent
(C) revived
(D) sighted
(E) antiquated

102. RIDICULE

(A) imitate
(B) try
(C) mock
(D) trap
(E) flog

103. DUAL

(A) swordfight
(B) tragic
(C) intersecting
(D) isolated
(E) two-fold

104. FLING

(A) steal
(B) toss
(C) enflame
(D) trip
(E) slide

105. POPULATE

(A) drain
(B) colonize
(C) relieve
(D) collate
(E) explode

106. INSTANTANEOUS

(A) punctuated
(B) sporadic
(C) immediate
(D) timely
(E) eventual

107. DEFT

(A) hard of hearing
(B) elusive
(C) bonkers
(D) adroit
(E) magical

108. CELESTIAL

(A) heavenly
(B) astrological
(C) meteorological
(D) cloudy
(E) underwater

109. BARBED

(A) bearded
(B) burnished
(C) trimmed
(D) coarse
(E) thorny

110. SUSPEND

(A) delay
(B) invoke
(C) glide
(D) accept
(E) flub

111. OFFICIAL

(A) tremendous
(B) valid
(C) fabricated
(D) triplicated
(E) repeated

112. NATURAL

(A) tainted
(B) contrived
(C) designed
(D) manipulated
(E) organic

113. DISSONANCE

(A) aloofness
(B) shame
(C) honor
(D) concordance
(E) disagreement

114. SEVERE

(A) refined
(B) stormy
(C) harsh
(D) indignant
(E) fluffy

115. FRETFUL

(A) irritable
(B) maudlin
(C) haughty
(D) insincere
(E) designed

116. COWARDICE

(A) ardor
(B) timidity
(C) empathy
(D) kindness
(E) complacency

117. ERA

(A) tall building
(B) historical event
(C) annual celebration
(D) time period
(E) type of plane

118. SCALPEL

(A) skiing tool
(B) ticket seller
(C) top of one's head
(D) surgical knife
(E) ice scraper

119. TYPICAL

(A) reflective
(B) singular
(C) conventional
(D) anomalous
(E) create

120. BEAR

(A) naked
(B) hopeless
(C) forested
(D) carry
(E) exposed

121. ENCUMBER

(A) vegetable
(B) relieve
(C) inure
(D) retreat
(E) burden

122. WELCOME

(A) surmise
(B) greet
(C) strain
(D) depart
(E) point

123. MOXIE

(A) discouragement
(B) loftiness
(C) values
(D) spunk
(E) travail

124. MISCELLANEOUS

(A) expert
(B) sundry
(C) vetted
(D) compartmentalized
(E) inventoried

125. ROTUND

(A) roundabout
(B) healthy
(C) corpulent
(D) flattering
(E) ponderous

126. INNUMERABLE

(A) innumerate
(B) countless
(C) fractional
(D) countable
(E) infinitesimal

127. EQUITABLE

(A) just
(B) alluring
(C) exalted
(D) wavering
(E) judicial

128. INDICT

(A) to enter somewhere
(B) to lose weight
(C) to be fired from a job
(D) to charge a criminal
(E) to free someone or something

129. OCCUPY

(A) dread
(B) abdicate
(C) yield
(D) fill
(E) meander

130. QUARANTINE

(A) to station troops
(B) to divide in four
(C) to woo someone
(D) to isolate
(E) to miss expectations

131. FAMINE

(A) hunger
(B) memorial
(C) cornucopia
(D) feast
(E) drought

132. MALICIOUS

(A) disrespectful
(B) vengeful
(C) lupine
(D) accidental
(E) serendipitous

133. TRADE

(A) interests
(B) salary
(C) exchange
(D) evaluations
(E) inventory

134. HOSPITABLE

(A) cordial
(B) dire
(C) terrible
(D) contagious
(E) humid

135. PREDICAMENT

(A) forecast
(B) error
(C) quagmire
(D) success
(E) hypothesis

136. FATIGUE

(A) tiredness
(B) love
(C) paralysis
(D) disease
(E) obesity

137. ADDITIONAL

(A) fewer
(B) doubled
(C) reproduced
(D) hefty
(E) more

138. INSIDIOUS

(A) shy
(B) overt
(C) sneaky
(D) steadfast
(E) logical

139. VOUCH

(A) seal
(B) assure
(C) moisten
(D) hold
(E) undo

140. SACRED

(A) catty
(B) holy
(C) alluring
(D) haunted
(E) costly

141. GULLIBLE

(A) losing
(B) musing
(C) trusting
(D) pandering
(E) meandering

142. LIMBER

(A) frail
(B) muscular
(C) cramped
(D) rigid
(E) supple

143. SOMNOLENT

(A) hopeful
(B) drowsy
(C) reclined
(D) homesick
(E) jagged

144. ACQUIRE

(A) force
(B) confuse
(C) obtain
(D) rescind
(E) misunderstand

145. FIASCO

(A) appetizer
(B) momentous event
(C) organized event
(D) guide
(E) disaster

146. EXEMPLARY

(A) outstanding
(B) worthwhile
(C) pedagogical
(D) designed
(E) horrific

147. BERATE

(A) honor
(B) scold
(C) pay tax
(D) attack
(E) measure

148. EVOKE

(A) repress
(B) invoke
(C) oppress
(D) impress
(E) suppress

149. CONVALESCENCE

(A) infirmity
(B) aging
(C) lockdown
(D) shriveling
(E) healing

150. AMBIVALENT

(A) mixed feelings
(B) overdone
(C) apathetic
(D) ridiculous
(E) ambidextrous

151. DECREE

(A) college diploma
(B) unit of temperature
(C) type of dessert
(D) cooking oil
(E) command

152. VARIANCE

(A) difference
(B) vacillation
(C) polarization
(D) curvature
(E) altitude

153. RENDER

(A) tear
(B) depict
(C) cover
(D) oscillate
(E) desist

154. BULGE

(A) battle
(B) couch
(C) large ball
(D) sack
(E) swell

155. IMMACULATE

(A) flawed
(B) imperfect
(C) flawless
(D) amoral
(E) crippled

156. HEED

(A) listen
(B) wail
(C) shriek
(D) terrify
(E) run

157. INITIATE

(A) hold
(B) forego
(C) commence
(D) jar
(E) wind

158. PRESAGE

(A) preview
(B) translate
(C) predict
(D) bother
(E) convey

159. DETER

(A) undergird
(B) check
(C) expel
(D) escape
(E) smell

160. THRIVE

(A) splice
(B) toil
(C) falter
(D) blossom
(E) exhaust

161. PROPAGANDA

(A) information to promote a particular viewpoint
(B) a large buffet
(C) piece for a stage in theater
(D) fancy restaurant with big menu and neon lighting
(E) something that buttresses

162. FRIVOLOUS

(A) detailed
(B) threadbare
(C) decorated
(D) wasteful
(E) earnest

163. ESSENTIAL

(A) cheap
(B) bizarre
(C) vital
(D) defective
(E) handmade

164. INADVERTANT

(A) absolute
(B) unintentional
(C) famous
(D) lucid
(E) careful

165. TREPIDATION

(A) fear
(B) anticipation
(C) alacrity
(D) envy
(E) astonishment

166. CHERISH

(A) trash
(B) encircle
(C) sweeten
(D) cosset
(E) blemish

167. HENCHMAN

(A) car mechanic
(B) wise mentor
(C) unscrupulous supporter
(D) local handyman
(E) childhood friend

168. FELON

(A) majestic bird
(B) fencing sword
(C) fairytale demon
(D) royal person
(E) criminal

169. REPRESS

(A) discard
(B) touch again
(C) heat
(D) flatten
(E) muffle

170. DILIGENT

(A) tardy
(B) fragmented
(C) calculated
(D) industrious
(E) evocative

171. ACCENTUATE

(A) mispronounce
(B) idealize
(C) gnaw
(D) exaggerate
(E) crush

172. WITHER

(A) mend
(B) bifurcate
(C) atrophy
(D) deride
(E) infuse

173. FORESTALL

(A) enervate
(B) encircle
(C) hinder
(D) cancel
(E) die out

174. ERODE

(A) deteriorate
(B) enliven
(C) thicken
(D) trod
(E) awaken

175. EXORBITANT

(A) removed
(B) foul
(C) excessive
(D) undervalued
(E) kitsch

176. SLUGGARD

(A) overweight person
(B) skilled baseball player
(C) large drink
(D) lazy person
(E) underground animal

177. VARIETY

(A) laughter
(B) assortment
(C) narrative
(D) excitement
(E) monotony

178. INCOHERENT

(A) parsed
(B) florid
(C) cogent
(D) germane
(E) jumbled

179. CONFUSION

(A) disorientation
(B) forgetfulness
(C) thoughtfulness
(D) tidiness
(E) order

180. EXONERATE

(A) to entangle
(B) to arrest
(C) to mince
(D) to venerate
(E) to free from blame

181. WINCE

(A) to draw back
(B) to have a victory
(C) to cleanse
(D) to tamper with
(E) to reshape

182. AGGRANDIZE

(A) to become famous
(B) to assess someone's honesty
(C) to start a business
(D) to divest
(E) to make seem bigger or greater

183. YIELD

(A) to grant
(B) to fear
(C) to waver
(D) to demand
(E) to use

184. RATIONAL

(A) organized
(B) dissuading
(C) logical
(D) convincing
(E) numerical

185. UNDERMINE

(A) measure
(B) obey
(C) drop
(D) scoop
(E) weaken

186. NOISOME

(A) irritating
(B) shrilly
(C) having an unpleasant odor
(D) loud
(E) bland

187. HARROWING

(A) simple
(B) time-consuming
(C) dynamic
(D) holy
(E) distressing

188. INTERCEPT

(A) punch
(B) volley
(C) seize
(D) pass
(E) throw

189. SANITARY

(A) lopsided
(B) disheveled
(C) fibrous
(D) clean
(E) humid

190. ANONYMOUS

(A) poetic
(B) decorated
(C) unnamed
(D) choreographed
(E) ordered

191. MURKY

(A) pure
(B) obscure
(C) creamy
(D) contaminated
(E) blatant

192. CONVENIENT

(A) momentous
(B) useful
(C) always open
(D) friendly
(E) extraneous

193. FALLACIOUS

(A) frank
(B) twisted
(C) well-dressed
(D) innocent
(E) untrue

194. RESIDUAL

(A) purposeful
(B) fundamental
(C) leftover
(D) continual
(E) enervating

195. CONTEMPORARY

(A) dated
(B) staged
(C) illusory
(D) realistic
(E) modern

196. PRIMITIVE

(A) alone
(B) insufficient
(C) basic
(D) plain
(E) forested

197. NOXIOUS

(A) dreamy
(B) toxic
(C) fulfilling
(D) tolerable
(E) offensive

198. DIVERSE

(A) different
(B) disorganized
(C) rumpled
(D) jumbled
(E) homogeneous

199. LACERATION

(A) bind
(B) grimace
(C) lace
(D) smirk
(E) cut

200. NEGLIGENT

(A) panicked
(B) dutiful
(C) wise
(D) dumb
(E) careless

201. INSINUATE

(A) avoid
(B) warn
(C) suggest
(D) query
(E) distrust

202. DETRIMENTAL

(A) intimidating
(B) damaging
(C) natural
(D) satisfying
(E) realistic

203. BUFFER

(A) acid
(B) solution
(C) cushion
(D) breakup
(E) accumulation

204. WEATHER

(A) tolerate
(B) endure
(C) fear
(D) enlarge
(E) omit

205. VOGUE

(A) urban
(B) exotic
(C) unclear
(D) fashionable
(E) rural

206. ENIGMA

(A) chart
(B) mythical creature
(C) folktale
(D) mystery
(E) maze

207. RECOGNIZE

(A) loathe
(B) notice
(C) think
(D) ensnare
(E) camouflage

208. ASCERTAIN

(A) disperse
(B) organize
(C) alphabetize
(D) locate
(E) determine

209. STIFLE

(A) suppress
(B) avoid
(C) rely
(D) divert
(E) encourage

210. EXPRESS

(A)   indirect
(B)   speedy
(C)   authentic
(D)   slow
(E)   ambiguous

211. WARRANT

(A)   blockade
(B)   authorization
(C)   notice
(D)   tease
(E)   modification

212. THOROUGH

(A)   concise
(B)   abundant
(C)   familiar
(D)   all-encompassing
(E)   atypical

213. COMMERCE

(A)   studies
(B)   business
(C)   organization
(D)   relationship
(E)   mood

214. PRESUMPTUOUS

(A)   selfless
(B)   selfish
(C)   self-confident
(D)   self-loathing
(E)   self-effacing

215. OPERATE

(A) call
(B) construct
(C) function
(D) oil
(E) fix

216. MATURE

(A) adolescent
(B) grown-up
(C) geriatric
(D) unseasoned
(E) measured

217. STATURE

(A) sincerity
(B) price
(C) volume
(D) prominence
(E) width

218. ROBUST

(A) rounded
(B) flourishing
(C) flimsy
(D) robotic
(E) mechanical

219. MANEUVER

(A) tactic
(B) restriction
(C) terror
(D) surrender
(E) defeat

220. DIMINISH

(A) decrease
(B) stir
(C) release
(D) inspire
(E) augment

221. CONCOCT

(A) redo
(B) erase
(C) decompose
(D) formulate
(E) feast

222. BEDLAM

(A) insomnia
(B) chaos
(C) resolution
(D) assuredness
(E) sleep

223. ADVERSITY

(A) inclination
(B) harsh attitude
(C) suspense
(D) setback
(E) creativity

224. TRANSPARENT

(A) handy
(B) obvious
(C) invisible
(D) gauzy
(E) opaque

225. PITHY

(A) carnal
(B) laconic
(C) arid
(D) seedy
(E) liminal

226. SATIATE

(A) panic
(B) satisfy
(C) starve
(D) displease
(E) taste yummy

227. SUBDUE

(A) demean
(B) purify
(C) crush
(D) exacerbate
(E) admire

228. DOMICILE

(A) cruise
(B) safari
(C) human habitat
(D) prison
(E) vehicle

229. STERN

(A) relaxed
(B) nervous
(C) strict
(D) seafaring
(E) traveled

230. TRIVIAL

(A) saucy
(B) plentiful
(C) unimportant
(D) cerebral
(E) mystery

231. VERIFY

(A) check
(B) unearth
(C) tell the truth
(D) bleed
(E) inquire

232. OBLIGATED

(A) required
(B) elongated
(C) gracious
(D) definite
(E) estranged

233. LIBERATE

(A) drown
(B) muffle
(C) suppress
(D) free
(E) crucify

234. FLABBERGASTED

(A) derailed
(B) married
(C) surprised
(D) hurt
(E) frightened

235. HUMBLE

(A) bloated
(B) moldy
(C) egocentric
(D) hungry
(E) unassuming

236. SEDATE

(A) silky
(B) synthetic
(C) adventurous
(D) staid
(E) frenzied

237. SWARTHY

(A) evil
(B) committed
(C) dark-complexioned
(D) infected
(E) pallid

238. GELID

(A) cubical
(B) frozen
(C) oozing
(D) fluorescent
(E) liquid

239. INQUISITIVE

(A) curious
(B) meaningful
(C) unending
(D) instructive
(E) neutral

240. PLENTIFUL

(A) empty
(B) abundant
(C) abnormal
(D) sufficient
(E) dearth

241. INTELLECTUAL

(A) aware
(B) organized
(C) artistic
(D) creative
(E) cerebral

242. CORRUPT

(A) rude
(B) belligerent
(C) illegal
(D) moral
(E) dishonest

243. DEFUNCT

(A) inoperative
(B) uncool
(C) functional
(D) valuable
(E) archaic

244. BRAZEN

(A) loopy
(B) thoughtful
(C) brash
(D) hasty
(E) fatigued

245. COMPEL

(A) repel
(B) expel
(C) impel
(D) rest
(E) deregulate

246. SUPREME

(A) tasty
(B) ignorant
(C) obsequious
(D) great
(E) large

247. REQUISITION

(A) suggestion to quit
(B) intense questioning
(C) demand for materials
(D) request for advice
(E) fear of sleep

248. BLOATED

(A) deficient
(B) sickly
(C) lean
(D) abnormal
(E) turgid

249. SYNOPSIS

(A) hypnosis
(B) diagnosis
(C) prescription
(D) summary
(E) excuse

250. ABYSS

(A) summit
(B) plateau
(C) incline
(D) decline
(E) chasm

251. COLOSSUS

(A) giant thing
(B) pebble
(C) statue
(D) odorless gas
(E) inventory

252. ODIOUS

(A) smelly
(B) blaring
(C) ruffled
(D) horrible
(E) stained

253. NEBULOUS

(A) lucid
(B) lenient
(C) weird
(D) vague
(E) sudden

254. HYPOCRISY

(A) deceitfulness
(B) piousness
(C) candor
(D) honesty
(E) rancor

255. UNILATERAL

(A) indecisive
(B) stymied
(C) roundabout
(D) turbulent
(E) one-sided

256. PURSUIT

(A) path
(B) chase
(C) fancy clothing
(D) costume
(E) carton

257. ANNIHILATE

(A) shape
(B) redirect
(C) congratulate
(D) acclaim
(E) destroy

258. SUBSIDY

(A) payment
(B) cost
(C) warrant
(D) proxy
(E) degree

259. INVINCIBLE

(A) impossible
(B) invulnerable
(C) indefensible
(D) mortal
(E) esoteric

260. REVELATION

(A) comedy
(B) portrayal
(C) malady
(D) disclosure
(E) omission

261. EGRESS

(A) stairwell
(B) ramp
(C) entryway
(D) digress
(E) exit

262. TRAUMATIC

(A) redeeming
(B) amazing
(C) ponderable
(D) insouciant
(E) frightening

263. PONDER

(A) berate
(B) proclaim
(C) exclaim
(D) consider
(E) reject

264. BARREN

(A) caged
(B) visible
(C) empty
(D) spacious
(E) furry

265. INDIGNATION

(A) humor
(B) relief
(C) anger
(D) thrill
(E) sentimentality

266. LULL

(A) dent
(B) disorder
(C) bump
(D) calm
(E) maelstrom

267. AMITY

(A) competition
(B) concern
(C) greediness
(D) silliness
(E) friendship

268. PRAGMATIC

(A) practical
(B) automatic
(C) ethereal
(D) noisy
(E) simple

269. IMITATE

(A) mirror
(B) idolize
(C) respect
(D) control
(E) defame

270. PALTRY

(A) lonely
(B) evacuated
(C) filling
(D) substantial
(E) meager

271. WHET

(A) steam
(B) crease
(C) undulate
(D) blunt
(E) sharpen

272. ATONE

(A) mock
(B) speak poetically
(C) sing
(D) apologize
(E) defeat

273. CULTIVATE

(A) adhere
(B) unite
(C) spin
(D) downplay
(E) nourish

274. PROSPEROUS

(A) essential
(B) galactic
(C) thriving
(D) blockaded
(E) revolving

275. TRADITION

(A) border
(B) custom
(C) holiday
(D) ignorance
(E) finality

276. DEBRIS

(A) gentle gale
(B) type of cheese
(C) tall building
(D) waste
(E) tools

277. PLAUSIBLE

(A) believable
(B) gullible
(C) wasteful
(D) ethical
(E) incredible

278. LANGUID

(A) lasting
(B) curious
(C) opinionated
(D) sluggish
(E) enthralled

279. RUDIMENTARY

(A) basic
(B) understandable
(C) involved
(D) arcane
(E) sophisticated

280. COMMENDABLE

(A) useless
(B) miserable
(C) laudable
(D) mandatory
(E) optional

281. PROGRESSIVE

(A) apolitical
(B) anarchical
(C) conservative
(D) liberal
(E) moderate

282. DETOUR

(A) slope
(B) line
(C) repetition of something
(D) indirect course
(E) voyage

283. CONTUSION

(A) bruise
(B) ache
(C) demand
(D) virus
(E) burst

284. TENACIOUS

(A) lax
(B) independent
(C) harsh
(D) loud
(E) stubborn

285. INSTIGATE

(A) terminate
(B) move
(C) play
(D) provoke
(E) quell

286. PRECARIOUS

(A) immature
(B) reasonable
(C) organized
(D) unstable
(E) odd

287. STOLID

(A) irritable
(B) mawkish
(C) impecunious
(D) impassive
(E) outraged

288. STATUTE

(A) mold
(B) token
(C) sculpture
(D) violation
(E) law

289. NULLIFY

(A) inscribe
(B) empower
(C) rescind
(D) swell
(E) validate

290. GOODWILL

(A) hopes
(B) firmness
(C) listlessness
(D) generosity
(E) miserliness

291. EVICT

(A) to warn wary travelers
(B) to throw out from a residence
(C) to charge a criminal with a crime
(D) to avoid a problem
(E) to be sent to prison

292. REJUVENATE

(A) implode
(B) pause
(C) omit
(D) obstruct
(E) revitalize

293. YEARN

(A) snore
(B) breathe
(C) tremble
(D) long
(E) divorce

294. GOAD

(A) evade
(B) assist
(C) move
(D) relax
(E) provoke

295. OSTENTATIOUS

(A) austerity
(B) clumsy
(C) adroit
(D) showy
(E) blind

296. BLISS

(A) flavor
(B) insipidness
(C) trembling
(D) joy
(E) somber

297. ORATION

(A) vacation
(B) poem
(C) speech
(D) choir
(E) dental tool

298. FEIGN

(A) tranquilize
(B) ache
(C) ignore
(D) pretend
(E) forget

299. BOISTEROUS

(A) stilted
(B) garbled
(C) mumbling
(D) tacit
(E) loud

300. FRUITFUL

(A) nutritious
(B) repetitive
(C) colorful
(D) productive
(E) zany

301. WAYWARD

(A) compliant
(B) unmanageable
(C) emotive
(D) plastic
(E) pliable

302. IMPOSE

(A) engage
(B) ape
(C) loosen
(D) recreate
(E) levy

303. COSMIC

(A) grandiose
(B) lunar
(C) tidal
(D) arboreal
(E) oceanic

304. PRECOCIOUS

(A) petulant
(B) inexplicable
(C) mature
(D) slovenly
(E) courageous

305. SECURE

(A) loose
(B) erratic
(C) atypical
(D) safe
(E) destabilized

306. HERCULEAN

(A) mighty
(B) unadorned
(C) basic
(D) indefensible
(E) imploding

307. FELON

(A) type of bird
(B) criminal
(C) moderator
(D) policeman
(E) judge

308. CONFIDENTIAL

(A) invasive
(B) secret
(C) open
(D) divulged
(E) harmonious

309. WANE

(A) dine
(B) flourish
(C) wax
(D) alcoholic drink
(E) ebb

310. EXTRACT

(A) twist
(B) remove
(C) intoxicate
(D) swindle
(E) roil

311. TURBULENT

(A) placid
(B) unstable
(C) unmoving
(D) gliding
(E) ordinary

312. VIVACIOUS

(A) lifeless
(B) curvy
(C) succulent
(D) exuberant
(E) dry

313. JUBILANT

(A) cute
(B) timorous
(C) elated
(D) saturnine
(E) convoluted

314. ECONOMICAL

(A) costly
(B) recessive
(C) prudent
(D) simple
(E) outlined

315.   JEOPARDY

(A)   trivia
(B)   peril
(C)   thrill
(D)   party
(E)   humor

ANALOGIES

The following questions ask you to find relationships between words. For each question, select the answer that best completes the meaning of the sentence.

1.   Lion is to pride as:

(A)   wolf is to pack
(B)   school is to fish
(C)   Siamese is to cat
(D)   rooster is to hen
(E)   joey is to kangaroo

2.   Dusk is to night as:

(A)   star is to sky
(B)   arid is to dry
(C)   moist is to wet
(D)   water is to fountain
(E)   shelf is to book

3.   Linguine is to noodle as:

(A)   cheddar is to cheese
(B)   nut is to shell
(C)   poached is to pear
(D)   stamen is to flower
(E)   pea is to pod

4.   Erudite is to reading as:

(A)   cosmopolitan is to traveling
(B)   starving is to cooking
(C)   sedated is to researching
(D)   flagging is to charging
(E)   deserted is to filling

5.   Gangway is to ship as:

(A)   subway is to metropolis
(B)   jetway is to airplane
(C)   highway is to travel
(D)   odometer is to car
(E)   pedal is to bike

6.   Premeditated is to arbitrary as:

(A)   blueprinted is to sketched
(B)   definite is to organized
(C)   outlined is to executed
(D)   random is to chance
(E)   designed is to impromptu

7.   Train is to depot as:

(A)   plane is to airport
(B)   ocean is to boat
(C)   car is to garage
(D)   truck is to truck stop
(E)   ship is to propeller

8.   Prong is to fork as:

(A)   tooth is to comb
(B)   teaspoon is to tablespoon
(C)   drip is to pour
(D)   one is to many
(E)   holder is to utensil

9.   Slim is to gaunt as:

(A)   heavy is to overweight
(B)   thin is to fat
(C)   pudgy is to obese
(D)   starving is to emaciated
(E)   rotund is to porcine

10.   Abridge is to truncate as:

(A)   sequel is to movie
(B)   stanza is to poem
(C)   redo is to effort
(D)   expand is to elaborate
(E)   heading is to chapter

11.   Read is to skim as:

(A)   whiff is to smell
(B)   wash is to dry
(C)   yawn is to sleep
(D)   wheeze is to cough
(E)   stare is to glance

12.   Clever is to fox as:

(A)   humane is to rabbit
(B)   elephant is to dumb
(C)   duck is to loony
(D)   cute is to pig
(E)   wise is to owl

13.   Quack is to doctor as:

(A)   counterfeit is to authentic
(B)   hostess is to stewardess
(C)   manager is to director
(D)   pedestrian is to jaywalker
(E)   mime is to actor

14. Soliloquy is to dialogue as:

(A) playwright is to conversation
(B) loneliness is to liveliness
(C) theater is to nonfiction
(D) one is to two
(E) apathy is to compassion

15. Troupe is to actor as:

(A) cousin is to brother
(B) employee is to company
(C) choir is to singer
(D) auditorium is to chairs
(E) film is to theater

16. Tremor is to earthquake as:

(A) folly is to silliness
(B) expurgation is to cancellation
(C) zephyr is to gale
(D) soup is to salad
(E) screech is to outcry

17. Autocracy is to oligarchy as:

(A) executive is to legislative
(B) self-control is to chaos
(C) government is to economics
(D) solo is to team
(E) automatic is to programmed

18. Harvest is to crop as:

(A) glean is to information
(B) pare is to reduce
(C) duplicate is to notes
(D) arrange is to clothing
(E) partition is to room

19.   Pliers are to electrician as:

(A)   taxicab is to driver
(B)   stethoscope is to doctor
(C)   nurse is to midwife
(D)   photographer is to camera
(E)   circuit is to wire

20.   Discrete is to continuous as:

(A)   number is to equation
(B)   detective is to crime
(C)   juice is to fruit
(D)   bricks are to water
(E)   birds are to bees

21.   Secret is to divulge as:

(A)   idea is to enclose
(B)   gossip is to murmur
(C)   crime is to squeal
(D)   hyena is to laugh
(E)   knowledge is to multiply

22.   Trash can is to receptacle as:

(A)   copper is to conductor
(B)   van is to haul
(C)   house is to key
(D)   microphone is to speaker
(E)   school is to teacher

23.   Patent is to invention as:

(A)   fax is to triplicate
(B)   certify is to invalidate
(C)   signify is to idol
(D)   check is to endorse
(E)   copyright is to writing

24. Prime is to divisor as:

(A) binary is to digit
(B) fraction is to decimal
(C) composite is to multiple
(D) part is to whole
(E) odd is to even

25. Kerosene is to lamp as:

(A) diesel is to truck
(B) octane is to unleaded
(C) clarity is to turbidity
(D) fruit is to sugar
(E) vegetables are to diet

26. Toss is to hurl as:

(A) tilt is to incline
(B) nosh is to snack
(C) nudge is to shove
(D) grip is to hold
(E) wind is to spin

27. Diplomacy is to offensiveness:

(A) affectation is to sincerity
(B) greed is to money
(C) altruism is to heart
(D) health is to excitement
(E) creativity is to ideas

28. Compass is to circle as:

(A) ruler is to line
(B) angle is to protractor
(C) ellipse is to parabola
(D) needle is to spin
(E) north is to pole

29. Raccoon is to nocturnal as:

(A) hawk is to aerial
(B) monkey is to arboreal
(C) snail is to terrestrial
(D) elephant is to diurnal
(E) squirrel is to eternal

30. Incendiary is to conflict as:

(A) wet is to ringing
(B) sinking is to floating
(C) crumbling is to burning
(D) indulging is to labor
(E) disturbing is to commotion

31. Excommunicate is to church as:

(A) banish is to country
(B) pledge is to fraternity
(C) oath is to citizenship
(D) pray is to pilgrimage
(E) child is to disinherit

32. Latin is to letter as:

(A) Spanish is to fiesta
(B) English is to universal
(C) French is to romance
(D) Chinese is to character
(E) Greek is to reason

33. Finch is to bird as:

(A) piranha is to flesh
(B) parrot is to jungle
(C) fish is to trout
(D) cobra is to snake
(E) clown is to circus

34. Yellow is to primary as:

(A) black is to darkness
(B) blue is to tertiary
(C) purple is to royal
(D) green is to secondary
(E) red is to warning

35. Cake is to tiers as:

(A) frosting is to layers
(B) ladder is to rungs
(C) gear is to speeds
(D) truffles are to sweets
(E) flour is to batters

36. Karate is to dojo as:

(A) hockey is to puck
(B) sensei is to black belt
(C) racquetball is to court
(D) ring is to boxing
(E) ball is to bocce

37. Maroon is to person as:

(A) jettison is to object
(B) color is to hue
(C) amass is to animal
(D) resist is to valuables
(E) swarm is to buccaneer

38. Trundle is to clumsy as:

(A) sashay is to flamboyant
(B) gallop is to disappointed
(C) limp is to elegant
(D) lunge is to coward
(E) crawl is to childish

39.   Petrify is to shock as:

(A)   retard is to hurry
(B)   decay is to freshen
(C)   enrapture is to delight
(D)   order is to reject
(E)   index is to find

40.   Magician is to legerdemain as:

(A)   robber is to apprehension
(B)   barista is to coffee
(C)   dentist is to teeth
(D)   athlete is to brains
(E)   psychic is to clairvoyance

41.   Underground is to stratosphere as:

(A)   spelunker is to pilot
(B)   worm is to spider
(C)   bunker is to tree house
(D)   home is to cloud
(E)   sink is to pinnacle

42.   Buff is to shine as:

(A)   chill is to freeze
(B)   conceal is to wrap
(C)   heal is to sully
(D)   poison to vitalize
(E)   mar is to disfigure

43.   Seductive is to siren as:

(A)   humility is to prima donna
(B)   married is to dowager
(C)   cacophonous is to diva
(D)   quarrelsome is to vixen
(E)   beautiful is to hag

44. Youth is to agedness as:

(A) senior is to junior
(B) medicine is to illness
(C) sunrise is to sunset
(D) marriage is to graduation
(E) newborn is to childhood

45. Schism is to fracture as:

(A) wedding is to union
(B) egg is to powder
(C) tape is to glue
(D) waif is to bony
(E) fixation is to myopia

46. yahoo is to unmannered:

(A) dreamer is to unimaginative
(B) reprobate is to unprincipled
(C) genius is to unintelligent
(D) expert is to unskilled
(E) professor is to uneducated

47. Heterogeneous is to diverse as:

(A) rocky is to sturdy
(B) undulating is to flat
(C) jumbled is to sorted
(D) polarized is to integrated
(E) constant is to unchanging

48. Archer is to bow and arrows as:

(A) detective is to magnifying glass
(B) fireman is to helmet
(C) plumber is to snake
(D) policeman is to badge
(E) sniper is to rifle

49.   Narcissism is to self as:

(A)   abnegation is to control
(B)   asceticism is to objects
(C)   manners are to etiquette
(D)   food is to gluttony
(E)   cupidity is to money

50.   Troublesome is to convenient:

(A)   transparent is to diaphanous
(B)   organized is to tidy
(C)   sweet is to saccharine
(D)   vexing is to satisfying
(E)   seductive is to tempting

51.   Chopsticks are to eating as:

(A)   ladle is for slurping
(B)   staple gun is to attacking
(C)   pencil is to writing
(D)   awl is to scratching
(E)   spoon is to drinking

52.   Natural is to synthetic as:

(A)   coloring is to food
(B)   silk is to polyester
(C)   lumber is to furniture
(D)   wool is to sheep
(E)   elastic is to stretchy

53.   Plaintiff is to defendant as:

(A)   lord is to vassal
(B)   winner is to loser
(C)   judge is to magistrate
(D)   basket is to hoop
(E)   offense is to defense

54.   Molar is to tooth as

(A)   fibula is to bone
(B)   strand is to hair
(C)   nostril is to nose
(D)   lash is to eye
(E)   taste is to mouth

55.   Cylinder is to circle as:

(A)   sphere is to round
(B)   cone is to point
(C)   triangular is to prism
(D)   pyramid is to edge
(E)   cube is to square

56.   Appetizer is to dessert as:

(A)   cake is to hors d'oeuvre
(B)   finale is to preview
(C)   anniversary is to wedding
(D)   commencement is to midterms
(E)   preface is to epilogue

57.   Pope is to Catholicism as:

(A)   Czar is to Russia
(B)   rock star is to pop culture
(C)   President is to America
(D)   Emperor is to China
(E)   Dalai Lama is to Tibetan Buddhism

58.   Drought is to flood as:

(A)   seriousness is to focus
(B)   nervousness is to anxiety
(C)   serene is to calm
(D)   feud is to quarrel
(E)   dearth is to excess

59. Spit is to meat as:

(A) microwave is to toast
(B) brick oven is to pizza
(C) freezer is to gelato
(D) broil is to fish
(E) dice is to vegetables

60. Jack is to mechanic as:

(A) pail is to water
(B) Jill is to hill
(C) teacher is to apple
(D) electrician is to voltmeter
(E) saw is to lumberjack

61. Star is to planet as :

(A) fixed is to wandering
(B) twinkle is to sparkle
(C) near is to far
(D) familiar is to alien
(E) rocky is to gaseous

62. Gold is to winner as:

(A) accolades are to rewards
(B) consolation is to prize
(C) trophy is to team
(D) bronze is to third place
(E) silver is to loser

63: Katana is to sword as:

(A) moccasin is to shoe
(B) biography is to mystery
(C) rake is to shovel
(D) page is to book
(E) door is to knob

64. Impale is to puncture as

(A) staple is to bind
(B) cut is to mend
(C) lace is to string
(D) print is to shade
(E) bind is to rip

65. Fjord is to cliffs as:

(A) river is to flood
(B) plateau is to flat
(C) sandwich is to bread
(D) beach is to surfboards
(E) island is to bay

66. Immutable is to transient as:

(A) blossom is to bloom
(B) puerile is to juvenile
(C) heavy is to ponderous
(D) colorful is to vibrant
(E) progressing is to stagnant

67. Audition is to role as:

(A) interview is for job
(B) believe is to achieve
(C) reject is to decide
(D) practice is to attempt
(E) try is to succeed

68. Gypsy is to itinerant as:

(A) Bedouin is to grandparent
(B) homebody is to stationary
(C) aborigine is to urban
(D) youth is to unmotivated
(E) native is to voyaging

69. Grave is to presto as:

(A) beat is to rhythm
(B) measure is to staff
(C) piano is to forte
(D) death is to magic
(E) slow is to fast

70. Apples are to cider as:

(A) strawberries are to jam
(B) beer is to barley
(C) wheat is to rye
(D) grapes are to wine
(E) orange is to marmalade

71. Naïve is to seasoned as:

(A) learned is to unstudied
(B) old-timer is to tyro
(C) slave is to master
(D) rookie is to veteran
(E) newbie is to greenhorn

72. Concise is to rambling as:

(A) proofread is to extemporaneous
(B) simple is to intricate
(C) longwinded is to brief
(D) long is to short
(E) reasoned is to thorough

73. Elegy is to poem as:

(A) dirge is to song
(B) jazz is to disco
(C) tirade is to speech
(D) limerick is to riddle
(E) trick is to trap

74. Magic is to deceive as:

(A) writing is to read
(B) graduation is to study
(C) cooking is to feed
(D) brooding is to solve
(E) erect is to damage

75. Line is to ray as:

(A) lance is to shield
(B) bicycle is to wheel
(C) eraser is to pencil
(D) trapezoid is to rectangle
(E) circumference is to arc

76. Pituitary is to gland as:

(A) bone is to cartilage
(B) triceps are to muscle
(C) skin is to wrinkle
(D) organ is to artery
(E) vein is to blood

77. Sully is to immaculate as:

(A) damage is to destroyed
(B) vitiate is to pure
(C) wrinkled is to old
(D) fountain is to youth
(E) insult is to assist

78. Crooked is to honest as:

(A) intrepid is fearless
(B) armed is to dangerous
(C) meek is to shy
(D) bend is to vertex
(E) disingenuous is to truthful

79. lunar is to solar as:

(A) over is to under
(B) eclipse is to cover
(C) moon is to sun
(D) Saturn is to saturnine
(E) jovial is to Jupiter

80. Strange is to ludicrous as:

(A) straight is to curly
(B) scalding is to boiling
(C) irritated is to furious
(D) mercury is to silver
(E) inquisitive is to intrigued

81. Grizzly is to hibernate as:

(A) swallow is to migrate
(B) monarch is to fly
(C) trump is to win
(D) hare is to rabbit
(E) corgi is to bark

82. Bland is to flavor as:

(A) ire is to creativity
(B) cute is to attractiveness
(C) languid is to zest
(D) pungent is to smell
(E) spice is to pepper

83. Discordance is to harmony as:

(A) pandemonium is to order
(B) heat is to lukewarm
(C) autonomy is to self-control
(D) happiness is to excitement
(E) scientific is to explain

84. Sojourn is to reside as:

(A) doze is to sleep
(B) mix is to mash
(C) elaborate is to enumerate
(D) heal is to help
(E) prolong is to protract

85. Sage is to wise as:

(A) dunce is to imbecile
(B) geezer is to adulthood
(C) ogre is to beauty
(D) homely is to attractive
(E) nymph is to ogre

86. Nonchalance is to concern as:

(A) amoral is to ethics
(B) partisan is to bias
(C) apologetic is to emotion
(D) tragic is to unforgiving
(E) braveness is to bravado

87. Lily is to flower as:

(A) conifer is to deciduous
(B) dandelion is to petal
(C) bush is to berry
(D) oak is to elm
(E) palm is to tree

88. Caterpillar is to butterfly as:

(A) dog is to puppy
(B) tiger is to lion
(C) tadpole is to frog
(D) wolf is to fox
(E) kitten is to cat

89. Moist is to saturated as:

(A) crime is to misdemeanor
(B) noisy is to deafening
(C) soft is to silky
(D) creative is to ennui
(E) thick is to syrupy

90. Babble is to speak as:

(A) tidy is to clean
(B) eloquent is to speech
(C) mellifluous is to sound
(D) outline is to essay
(E) scattered is to thoughts

91. Satchel is to shoulder as:

(A) elbow is to kneecap
(B) back is to backpack
(C) fanny pack is to waist
(D) hand is to purse
(E) sandal is to sneaker

92. Footlong is to hot dog as:

(A) swivel is to rotate
(B) giant is to dwarf
(C) stack is to pancake
(D) limousine is to town car
(E) cheese is to hamburger

93. Hex is to witch as:

(A) hair is to barber
(B) order is to judge
(C) visit is to tourist
(D) building is to engineer
(E) muffin is to baker

94.   Equine is to lupine as:

(A)   horse is to wolf
(B)   fox is to cat
(C)   dog is to fish
(D)   cow is to bird
(E)   pig is to iguana

95.   Ambrosia is to taste as:

(A)   jarring is to sound
(B)   aromatic is to smell
(C)   eyesore is to sight
(D)   coarse is to smoothness
(E)   ponderous is to idea

96.   Prune is to plum as:

(A)   orange is to tangerine
(B)   apricot is to nectar
(C)   raisin is to grape
(D)   lemon is to lemonade
(E)   tomato is to potato

97.   Unicorn is to horse as:

(A)   monkey is to gorilla
(B)   Siamese is to cat
(C)   bull is to matador
(D)   phoenix is to bird
(E)   calf is to cow

98.   Butter is to churn as:

(A)   cocoa is to bean
(B)   milk is to utter
(C)   milkshake is to blender
(D)   cream is to opaque
(E)   left is to right

99.   Sigh is to relief as:

(A)   grimace is to glee
(B)   smirk is to humor
(C)   shriek is to fear
(D)   nap is to boredom
(E)   interest is to giggle

100. Lobbyist is to legislation as:

(A)   supervisor is to production
(B)   attorney is to verdict
(C)   retailer is to design
(D)   psychiatrist is to emotion
(E)   witness is to subpoena

101. Tariff is to import as:

(A)   export is to income
(B)   income is to tax
(C)   penalty is to fine
(D)   tithe is to churchgoer
(E)   bonus is to salary

102. Immigrate is to emigrate as:

(A)   amalgamate is to deplete
(B)   movement is to rest
(C)   deposit is to withdraw
(D)   rotate is to revolve
(E)   native is to alien

103. Quintuple is to five as:

(A)   octagon is to stop
(B)   single is to unique
(C)   quadruple is to six
(D)   double is to two
(E)   three is to tricycle

104. Brook is to river as:

(A)   spark is to conflagration
(B)   darkness is to light
(C)   roar is to meow
(D)   hint is to suggest
(E)   nourish is to grow

105. Moon is to Earth as:

(A)   electron is to nucleus
(B)   ring is to Saturn
(C)   sun is to asteroid
(D)   meteor is to meteorite
(E)   rotation is to axis

106. Sprint is to jog as:

(A)   saunter is to walk
(B)   gallop is to trot
(C)   skip is to jump
(D)   sit is to crawl
(E)   drive is to fly

107. Address is to home as:

(A)   license plate is to vehicle
(B)   traffic is to light
(C)   product is to bar code
(D)   surname is to forename
(E)   scanner is to price

108. Soprano is to bass as:

(A)   conductor is to musician
(B)   foreman is to boss
(C)   thief is to rob
(D)   escalator is to staircase
(E)   rise is to depression

109.   Request is to demand as:

(A)   beg is to plead
(B)   inquire is to ask
(C)   ecstatic is to happy
(D)   decline is to reject
(E)   hover is to sink

110.   Bobbin is to thread as:

(A)   sewing is to crochet
(B)   needle is to hole
(C)   spool is to pin
(D)   string is to cut
(E)   toilet paper is to roll

111.   Bird is to aviary as:

(A)   bee is to apiary
(B)   ant is to antennae
(C)   gopher is to hole
(D)   cage is to lion
(E)   dinosaur is to extinct

112.   Florid is to writing as:

(A)   spare is to edifice
(B)   paint is to chipping
(C)   ornate is to furniture
(D)   wood is to veneer
(E)   cow is to mottled

113.   Painting is to easel as:

(A)   drawing is to pencil
(B)   sculpture is to clay
(C)   column is to building
(D)   chalk is to pastel
(E)   camera is to tripod

114. Grade is to slope as:

(A) Celsius is to Fahrenheit
(B) calorie is to heat
(C) feet are to fathom
(D) sea is to ocean
(E) pulley is to lever

115. Husk is to corn as:

(A) wheat is to barley
(B) rind is to grapefruit
(C) pit is to peach
(D) seed is to grape
(E) skin is to apple

116. Vermillion is to red as:

(A) navy is to blue
(B) yellow is to golden
(C) magenta is to cyan
(D) emerald is to green
(E) black is to grey

117. Sharp is to flat as:

(A) sound is to crescendo
(B) hill is to valley
(C) spoon is to knife
(D) blunt is to pointy
(E) easy is to hard

118. Venison is to deer as:

(A) horn is to antler
(B) joey is to kangaroo
(C) coop is to chicken
(D) beef is to cow
(E) pig is to pork

119. Whip is to lash as:

(A) fire is to gun
(B) club is to bludgeon
(C) slay is to sword
(D) karate is to defend
(E) knife is to brandish

120. Year is to century as:

(A) penny is to dollar
(B) penny is to dime
(C) dollar is to dime
(D) dime is to quarter
(E) quarter is to nickel

121. Insulation is to cold as:

(A) photograph is to preserve
(B) water is to flood
(C) asbestos is to fire
(D) copper is to conduction
(E) acoustic is to sound

122. Vertigo is to nausea as:

(A) humidity is to storm
(B) smoking is to lung cancer
(C) cleverness is to dupe
(D) darkness is to visibility
(E) petroleum is to oil

123. Marathon is to win as:

(A) instruction is to research
(B) physician is to heal
(C) clown is to costume
(D) education is to teach
(E) sleeping is to working

124. Acidic is to basic as:

(A)   rudimentary is to simple
(B)   wet is to damp
(C)   red is to blue
(D)   repeated is to renovated
(E)   light is to darkness

125. Xylophone is to percussion as:

(A)   mallet is to gong
(B)   trumpet is to tuba
(C)   tympani is to drum
(D)   clarinet is to woodwind
(E)   brass is to saxophone

126. Migraine is to headache as:

(A)   influenza is to illness
(B)   hypothermia is to fever
(C)   torpor is to strength
(D)   energy is to exhaustion
(E)   chill is to fever

127. Rubber is to tires as:

(A)   pulp is to orange
(B)   denim is to jeans
(C)   cotton is to plant
(D)   handle is to door
(E)   cube is to squares

128. Artisanal is to hands as:

(A)   artificial is to natural
(B)   olfactory is to smell
(C)   eyes are to visual
(D)   mass-produced is to machine
(E)   acoustic is to ears

129. Altimeter is to height as:

(A)   current is to galvanometer
(B)   submarine is to depth
(C)   weather is to climate
(D)   nausea is to dizziness
(E)   pedometer is to steps

130. Abscess is to turgid as:

(A)   outlook is to myopic
(B)   relish is to cherish
(C)   night is to dark
(D)   mushroom is to fungus
(E)   abrasion is to worn

131. Religious is to secular as:

(A)   library is to learning
(B)   gym is to healthy
(C)   fire station is to emergency
(D)   post office is to busy
(E)   volatile is to stable

132. Quench is to hydrate as:

(A)   perplexity is to enlightenment
(B)   lose is to give
(C)   sate is to nourish
(D)   race is to velocity
(E)   starve is to feed

133. Recidivism is to crime as:

(A)   gambling is to earning
(B)   print is to book
(C)   filth is to cleanliness
(D)   confusion is to ideas
(E)   repetition is to words

134. Numerator is to denominator as:

(A)   attic is to basement
(B)   port is to starboard
(C)   kitchen is to bedroom
(D)   sink is to toilet
(E)   mirror is to reflection

135. Rust is to iron as:

(A)   mold is to cheese
(B)   aluminum is to alloy
(C)   banana is to rot
(D)   sparkle is to cleanly
(E)   sheen is to plastic

ANSWER KEY

SYNONYMS:

1.	B	41.	E	81.	D
2.	A	42.	E	82.	A
3.	D	43.	C	83.	E
4.	A	44.	A	84.	A
5.	B	45.	B	85.	D
6.	E	46.	C	86.	A
7.	E	47.	B	87.	E
8.	A	48.	E	88.	D
9.	C	49.	B	89.	A
10.	D	50.	D	90.	B
11.	A	51.	B	91.	C
12.	B	52.	C	92.	E
13.	B	53.	A	93.	C
14.	B	54.	A	94.	B
15.	E	55.	C	95.	E
16.	B	56.	C	96.	D
17.	D	57.	B	97.	A
18.	C	58.	D	98.	C
19.	C	59.	E	99.	A
20.	A	60.	C	100.	D
21.	D	61.	A	101.	B
22.	B	62.	E	102.	C
23.	E	63.	B	103.	E
24.	C	64.	E	104.	B
25.	C	65.	A	105.	B
26.	B	66.	D	106.	C
27.	B	67.	D	107.	D
28.	C	68.	E	108.	A
29.	A	69.	E	109.	E
30.	E	70.	C	110.	A
31.	B	71.	A	111.	B
32.	C	72.	A	112.	E
33.	B	73.	B	113.	E
34.	E	74.	D	114.	C
35.	D	75.	D	115.	A
36.	B	76.	C	116.	B
37.	D	77.	B	117.	D
38.	B	78.	E	118.	D
39.	B	79.	C	119.	C
40.	D	80.	D	120.	D

121.	E	167.	C	213.	B
122.	B	168.	E	214.	C
123.	D	169.	E	215.	C
124.	B	170.	D	216.	B
125.	C	171.	D	217.	D
126.	B	172.	C	218.	B
127.	A	173.	C	219.	A
128.	D	174.	A	220.	A
129.	D	175.	C	221.	D
130.	D	176.	D	222.	B
131.	A	177.	B	223.	D
132.	B	178.	E	224.	B
133.	C	179.	A	225.	B
134.	A	180.	E	226.	B
135.	C	181.	A	227.	C
136.	A	182.	E	228.	C
137.	E	183.	A	229.	C
138.	C	184.	C	230.	C
139.	B	185.	E	231.	A
140.	B	186.	C	232.	A
141.	C	187.	E	233.	D
142.	E	188.	C	234.	C
143.	B	189.	D	235.	E
144.	C	190.	C	236.	D
145.	E	191.	B	237.	C
146.	A	192.	B	238.	B
147.	B	193.	E	239.	A
148.	B	194.	C	240.	B
149.	E	195.	E	241.	E
150.	A	196.	C	242.	E
151.	E	197.	B	243.	A
152.	A	198.	A	244.	C
153.	B	199.	E	245.	C
154.	E	200.	E	246.	D
155.	C	201.	C	247.	C
156.	A	202.	B	248.	E
157.	C	203.	C	249.	D
158.	C	204.	B	250.	E
159.	B	205.	D	251.	A
160.	D	206.	D	252.	D
161.	A	207.	B	253.	D
162.	D	208.	E	254.	A
163.	C	209.	A	255.	E
164.	B	210.	B	256.	B
165.	A	211.	B	257.	E
166.	D	212.	D	258.	A

259.	B	278.	D	297.	C
260.	D	279.	A	298.	D
261.	E	280.	C	299.	E
262.	E	281.	D	300.	D
263.	D	282.	D	301.	B
264.	C	283.	A	302.	E
265.	C	284.	E	303.	A
266.	D	285.	D	304.	C
267.	E	286.	D	305.	D
268.	A	287.	D	306.	A
269.	A	288.	E	307.	B
270.	E	289.	C	308.	B
271.	E	290.	D	309.	E
272.	D	291.	B	310.	B
273.	E	292.	E	311.	B
274.	C	293.	D	312.	D
275.	B	294.	E	313.	C
276.	D	295.	D	314.	C
277.	A	296.	D	315.	B

ANALOGY SOLUTIONS:

1.	A		43.	D
2.	C		44.	C
3.	A		45.	A
4.	A		46.	B
5.	B		47.	E
6.	E		48.	E
7.	A		49.	E
8.	A		50.	D
9.	C		51.	C
10.	D		52.	B
11.	E		53.	E
12.	E		54.	A
13.	A		55.	E
14.	D		56.	E
15.	C		57.	E
16.	C		58.	E
17.	D		59.	B
18.	A		60.	C
19.	B		61.	A
20.	D		62.	D
21.	C		63.	D
22.	A		64.	A
23.	E		65.	C
24.	A		66.	E
25.	A		67.	A
26.	C		68.	B
27.	A		69.	E
28.	A		70.	D
29.	D		71.	D
30.	E		72.	B
31.	A		73.	A
32.	D		74.	C
33.	D		75.	B
34.	D		76.	B
35.	B		77.	B
36.	C		78.	E
37.	A		79.	C
38.	A		80.	C
39.	C		81.	A
40.	E		82.	C
41.	A		83.	A
42.	E		84.	A

85.	A		111.	A
86.	A		112.	C
87.	E		113.	E
88.	C		114.	B
89.	B		115.	B
90.	E		116.	D
91.	C		117.	B
92.	D		118.	D
93.	B		119.	B
94.	A		120.	A
95.	B		121.	C
96.	C		122.	B
97.	D		123.	B
98.	C		124.	E
99.	C		125.	D
100.	B		126.	A
101.	D		127.	B
102.	C		128.	D
103.	D		129.	E
104.	A		130.	E
105.	A		131.	E
106.	B		132.	C
107.	A		133.	E
108.	E		134.	A
109.	D		135.	A
110.	E			

HINTS FOR SOLVING ANALOGY QUESTIONS:

1. a pride is a group of lions
2. dusk is not completely dark; night is so
3. linguine is a type of noodle
4. one who is erudite likely does a lot of reading
5. a gangway is the raised platform one uses to board a ship
6. something that is premeditated is planned, something that is arbitrary is not
7. a train picks up and drops off passengers at a depot
8. a prong is a sharp pointed part of a fork
9. slim is thin, but gaunt is so thin you can see one's bones
10. to abridge and to truncate are both different ways of shortening something
11. to skim is to read without extreme depth or intensity
12. a fox is noted to be clever in folklore and stories
13. a quack is a person who claims to have medical knowledge but who is not truly a doctor
14. a soliloquy involves one speaker whereas a dialogue involves two speakers
15. a troupe is a group of actors
16. an earthquake is an earth tremor of great magnitude
17. an autocracy is a government system where one person has absolute power; an oligarchy is a government system where a small group of people have power
18. to harvest is to gather crops
19. pliers are used by an electrician
20. something that is discrete is breakable into countable parts, something that is continuous is not
21. to divulge is to tell an unknowing person or persons about a secret
22. a trash can is a kind of receptacle
23. a patent legally protects an invention
24. a number that is prime only has two divisors
25. kerosene is a type of fuel used to make a lamp work
26. to hurl is to toss forcefully
27. one who practices diplomacy avoids offensiveness
28. a compass is used to draw a circle
29. in terms of sleeping habits, a raccoon is a nocturnal animal
30. something that is incendiary tends to cause conflict
31. to excommunicate someone is to throw him or her out of the Church
32. the Latin language uses letters
33. a finch is a type of bird
34. yellow is a primary color
35. a cake (of many levels) is composed of tiers
36. karate is practiced in a dojo
37. to maroon is to abandon or discard a person or group of people
38. to trundle is to move slowly, clumsily, or unevenly

39. to petrify is to be extremely shocked
40. a magician uses legerdemain to perform his or her task
41. a spelunker works primarily underground while a pilot works primarily in the stratosphere
42. one buffs something in order to make it shine
43. a siren is a woman who is seductive
44. youth refers to a period at the beginning of life; agedness refers to a period advanced or at the end of life
45. a schism is a fracture
46. a yahoo is an unmannered person
47. something that is heterogeneous is diverse
48. an archer is someone who uses a bow (and arrows) to shoot a target
49. narcissism is a love for oneself
50. something that is troublesome is not convenient
51. chopsticks are utensils used for eating
52. silk is a natural fiber whereas polyester is a synthetic fiber
53. a plaintiff brings a case against a defendant in a court of law
54. a molar is a type of tooth
55. the base of a cylinder is a circle
56. an appetizer comes before a meal whereas a dessert comes after
57. the Pope is the head of Catholicism, a religious movement
58. a drought is too little rain; a flood is too much rain
59. meat is often cooked on a spit
60. a jack is a tool that can be used by a mechanic
61. a star is fixed in space whereas a planet moves through the sky
62. the winner of an event takes (a) gold (medal)
63. a katana is a type of sword
64. to impale is to puncture
65. a fjord is surrounded on both sides by cliffs
66. something that is immutable is not transient
67. one prepares for an audition with the hope of obtaining a role
68. a gypsy is a person who is associated with being itinerant
69. grave concerns music that is very slow paced, while presto is very fast paced
70. apples are used to make cider
71. one who is naïve is not experienced; one who is seasoned is very experienced
72. one who is concise uses few words, one who is rambling uses too many (and often incoherently)
73. an elegy is a poem lamenting the dead
74. the goal of magic is to deceive
75. a line is composed of two rays
76. the pituitary is a type of gland
77. to sully something is to make it immaculate no longer
78. someone who is crooked is not honest
79. something lunar concerns or is related to the moon; something that is solar concerns or is related to the sun
80. something ludicrous is extremely strange

81. a grizzly (bear) hibernates in winter
82. something bland lacks flavor
83. discordance concerns a lack of harmony
84. to sojourn is to stay somewhere for a short visit; to reside is to stay somewhere long term
85. someone who is a sage is considered to be wise
86. to possess nonchalance is to possess a lack of concern (for something)
87. a lily is a type of flower
88. a caterpillar morphs into a butterfly
89. something that is moist is a bit wet; something that is saturated is completely wet
90. to babble is to speak in a non-organized or nonsensical manner
91. a satchel is carried on one's shoulder
92. a footlong is an extremely long hot dog
93. a witch has the power to create and enforce a hex
94. equine concerns horses; lupine concerns wolves
95. ambrosia concerns something with a pleasant taste
96. a prune is a dried plum
97. a unicorn is a mythical type of horse
98. a churn is used to make butter
99. one makes a sigh as an indication of relief
100. the goal of a lobbyist is to attempt to influence legislation
101. a tariff is a tax imposed on imports
102. to immigrate is to move into a country; to emigrate is to move out of a country
103. a quintuple is five copies of something
104. a brook is like a tiny river (or tiny path of water)
105. the moon orbits the Earth
106. a sprint is to move very fast; to jog is to move somewhat fast
107. an address is a number (or series of numbers and letters) used to identify a house
108. a soprano has a high voice; a bass has a low voice
109. to request is to ask politely; to demand is to ask forcefully and authoritatively
110. thread is wound around a bobbin
111. an aviary is a large cage that can hold several kinds of birds
112. writing that is florid is colorful and elaborate
113. often a painting rests on an easel while it is being made
114. a grade is the measure of how steep or intense a slope is
115. the husk is the inedible part of corn one peels away before obtaining the edible part
116. vermillion is a bright red color
117. a musical sound that is sharp is above true or normal pitch; a musical sound that is flat is below true or normal pitch
118. venison is deer meat
119. one uses a whip to lash someone and injure him or her
120. a century is composed of one hundred years

121. insulation is material used to protect from cold
122. excessive vertigo can cause nausea
123. the goal of a marathon is to win
124. something that is acidic has a low pH; something that is basic has a high pH
125. a xylophone belongs to the group of percussion instruments
126. a migraine is a (serious) type of headache
127. tires are made of rubber
128. something artisanal is typically made with the hands
129. an altimeter is a tool that measures height
130. an abscess is turgid
131. something that is religious is not secular
132. to quench is to hydrate
133. recidivism is the tendency to repeat or commit the same crime again
134. a numerator is the number or value on the top of a fraction; a denominator is the number or value on the bottom of a fraction
135. rust is caused when iron is neglected and unused

ABOUT THE AUTHOR

Justin Grosslight is an academic entrepreneur interested in examining relationships between science and business. He is especially intrigued by how networks operate (quantitatively and qualitatively), both from historical and from contemporary perspectives. He holds degrees in history and mathematics from Stanford, a history of science degree from Harvard, and has published in all three fields. He is passionate about business, entertainment, academia, and writing, and enjoys helping talented youth thrive in their intellectual pursuits.

Justin has had years of experience in training students for their SAT®, SSAT®, ACT®, GMAT®, GRE®, AP® Calculus, IB® mathematics, SAT® physics subject test, and SAT® mathematics subject tests. He is a national merit scholar who received a perfect 800 on his SAT® math exam, perfect 800 on his SAT® math level 2 subject test, perfect 170 on his GRE® math exam, perfect 5 on his AP® Calculus BC exam (as a sophomore), perfect 5 on his AP® US History Exam, perfect 6 on his GMAT® writing exam, a perfect 8 on his GMAT® integrated reasoning exam, and near perfect scores on all of his other exams. He has published widely in both the humanities and in mathematics.

Several of Justin's students have received perfect scores on sections of their SAT® and ACT® exams, on their SAT® math subject test, and on their SAT® physics subject test. They have gained admission into prestigious universities such as Stanford University, NYU, UCLA, UC Berkeley, The University of Pennsylvania, and Oberlin College.

ABOUT JJMG ENTERPRISES LLC

Realizing that different students have different needs, JJMG Enterprises LLC believes that the best way to train students was to mentor them in both a personalized and intensive framework. Our aims are threefold:

1. To help students achieve test scores that will gain them admittance to universities of their choice

2. To develop writing, communication, quantitative, and analytical skills that will help students flourish in a global context

3. To instill values of character and responsibility in students that will help students succeed in their personal and professional endeavors

We also believe that many students and professionals can benefit from our books, so we have released them for sale to the public.

www.ingramcontent.com/pod-product-compliance
Lightning Source LLC
La Vergne TN
LVHW061248060426
835508LV00018B/1548